Magic
Tricks for
Kids

MAGIC TRICKS
FOR KIDS

Easy Step-by-Step Instructions for 25 Amazing Illusions

Phil Ackerly

Illustrated by Paul Borchers

ROCKRIDGE PRESS

Interior and Cover Designer: John Clifford
Art Producer: Tom Hood
Editor: Elizabeth Baird
Production Editor: Mia Moran
Illustrations © Paul Borchers 2020. Author photograph courtesy of Philip Goldworth.

ISBN: Print 978-1-64611-838-0 | eBook 978-1-64611-839-7
R0

*To my wife, Therese,
and son, Scott, who are the
real magic in my life.*

CONTENTS

A NOTE TO KIDS

Welcome to the wonderful world of magic! Between the covers of this book, you'll learn the secrets to a bunch of amazing magic tricks. Your job will be to perform them in an entertaining way, creating laughter, suspense, and surprise for everyone. It's an awesome opportunity, isn't it? And I know you can do it!

Where to begin? First, learn the beginner tricks. They are simple to do and will help you gain confidence. When you have mastered these tricks, then you are ready to learn the intermediate tricks. These require some **sleight of hand** skills (hiding objects in your hands). Finally, the advanced tricks will be waiting for you to master next. Here you will learn mind-reading tricks, card tricks, and how to make stuff appear out of thin air!

With each trick is a section called **PRACTICE TIME**. Here you learn how to do the secret moves before you are ready to perform for your audience. The more you practice, the less you have to think about what to do and say when you're in front of a crowd.

In the next section, **IT'S SHOWTIME**, you will learn what to say when you perform—what we call **patter**. What you say is also part of the magic. If your words are entertaining, then people will enjoy listening rather than trying to figure out how the tricks are done.

If you find any of the tricks hard to understand, that's okay! I didn't find all the tricks easy when I started learning magic, either. Put the hard trick aside and learn a different one. Then, in a week or two, or maybe a month, go back and try the harder trick again. Eventually, you'll be saying, "Hey, I get it now!"—just like I did when I was your age.

Most of the items you need can be found around the home. Be sure to ask your parents for permission before you use anything. And be sure to look at the **MAGICAL CRAFTS** section on how to make a magic wand, magic box, and magic table to help you put on fantastic shows. Always use extra caution when working with sharp objects such as scissors. Ask an adult for a safe pair intended for kids. And ask an adult for help making these tricks if you get stuck.

Above all, have fun! Remember, when you have fun, the audience will have fun, too!

A NOTE TO PARENTS

I've been teaching these magic tricks for over 25 years at summer camps, libraries, after-school programs, and private parties. The tricks in this book are all kid-tested and fun to perform. Some will challenge your child to learn new skills. As the tricks become more complex, they might even be challenging for you, too!

I always tell my students that magic is an art form, which combines theater, fine motor skills, public speaking, hand-eye coordination, memorization, math skills (that's right, math!), and planning. But the real art of magic is in the performance, the personality of the individual magician.

A good magician does not perform their magic to fool, but to *entertain* people. The magician's performance should tell a story. The performer is sharing a part of themselves with the audience. That's why the tricks in this book are accompanied by short scripts kids can learn to make their performance more engaging.

You may want to sit down with your child and learn the magic together. Help them understand the basic concepts of the tricks. If you child feels discouraged, please encourage them to keep practicing and performing. One thing you can do to help them is watch their performance and be amazed. If a sibling or one of your child's friends says things like, "I saw what you did," "I know how you did it," or "Let me see that," boost your child's confidence with your enthusiasm over their new skills. As they continue to practice, they will get better and better. And who knows, they may become a professional entertainer.

Above all, magic should be fun. For young children, it's not important for them to be able to "fool" their audience with the magic. The important part is that they are reading, building props, practicing, and memorizing lines of patter. They will gain confidence during the learning process and will begin to feel comfortable speaking and performing in front of others.

MAGICIAN'S CODE

PRACTICE MAKES PERFECT

Actually, practice, practice, practice makes perfect. You must promise
to practice until you can perform the trick with confidence. You can
only get good at something when you practice every day.
So, take small steps and practice these tricks
until you can perform them easily.

NEVER REPEAT THE SAME TRICK
TWICE TO THE SAME AUDIENCE

You should never perform the same trick twice because the audience
will already know how it works, and it will make it too easy for
them to figure out how it's done.

NEVER TELL
HOW THE TRICK IS DONE

Don't tell your friends how the trick works—it will only spoil the
surprise and make the magic less appealing. Once the secret is out,
there is no magic.

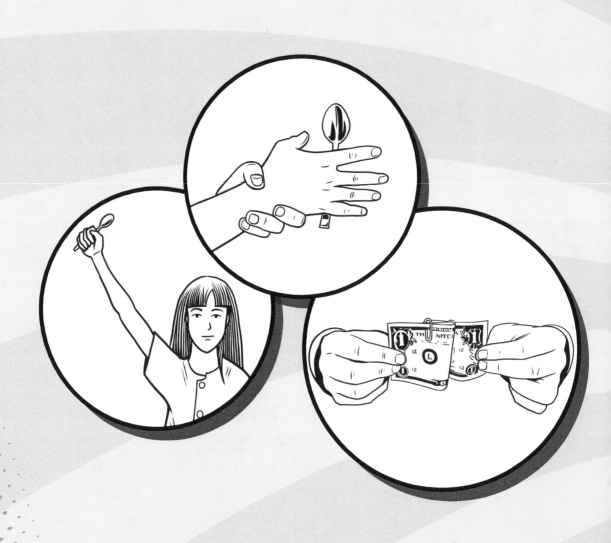

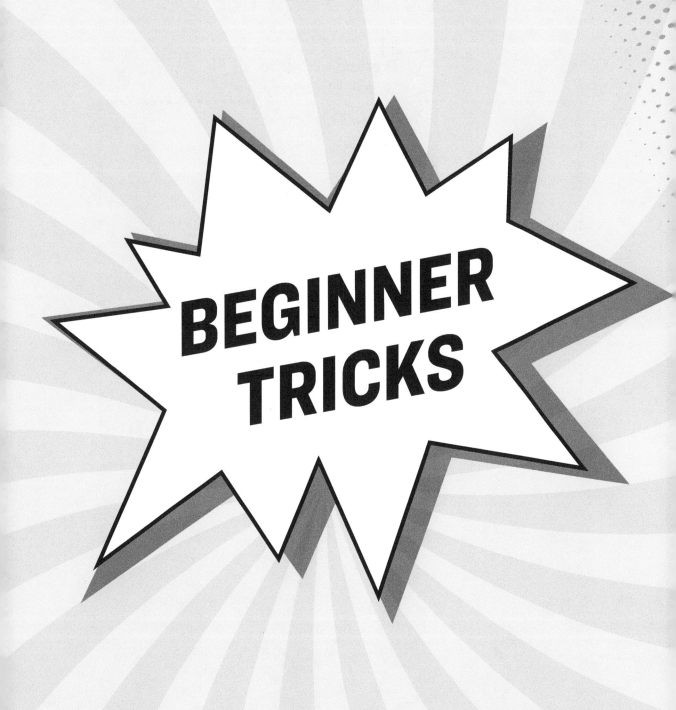

BEGINNER TRICKS

☆ STRAW SORCERY ☆

Pretend to Create Static Electricity

THE TRICK

A straw magically rolls across the table all by itself.

HOW DO YOU DO IT?

You blow on the straw to make it move. The audience thinks you are doing it with static electricity. Of course, you really don't create static electricity—it's just an **illusion**.

WHAT YOU'LL NEED

• A drinking straw (paper or plastic)

PRACTICE TIME

Hold your hand about 12 inches in front of your face. Gently blow on your hand, and notice that you can feel the air. Don't blow hard or make a sound, and try not to make an obvious "blowing" face. Just a gentle blow is all you need. This is how you will make the straw roll across the table. Practice in front of the mirror until you can do it with confidence. This is a great **impromptu** trick, meaning you can do it almost anywhere.

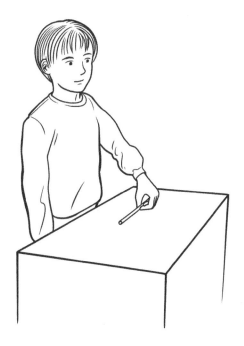

STEP 1

Lay the straw down on a table in front of you as shown in the illustration below.

Now stand behind the table. Find an imaginary spot about 4 to 6 inches behind the straw. This is where you aim when you blow. Remember to blow softly and quietly.

STEP 2

Start rubbing your finger in your hair, back and forth about 4 to 6 times. This is what you will do to pretend to "charge" it with static electricity.

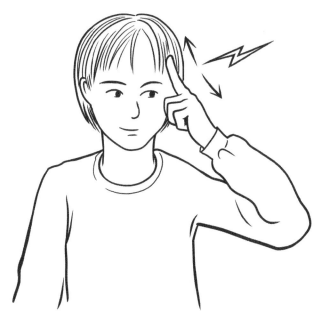

STEP 3

Point your "charged" finger at the straw and slowly move it around in a circle, while you blow on the straw just as you practiced earlier. Your breath will bounce off the table and onto the straw, causing it to roll away from you.

IT'S SHOWTIME!

Set the straw on the table. Hold up your first finger and say, "I will now create static electricity in my finger."

Rub your finger in your hair as you did in practice. Then hold your finger up, look at it, then look at the audience and say, "Now my finger is charged with electricity."

Point your finger at the straw and move your finger around in a small circle. Say, "Watch the straw!" This will get the audience to look at the straw and not your mouth. This is called **misdirection**—getting the audience to look where the magician wants them to look.

Now, give a gentle blow on the straw, making it roll away from you a few inches. When the straw begins to stop moving, say "Stop!"

To finish your first trick, look at the audience, rub your finger in your hair again, and add a joke like, "Who wants me to recharge their phone?"

Congratulations, you performed your first magic trick. Take a well-deserved bow!

☆ MAGNETIC HAND ☆

Look, Ma— No Hands!

THE TRICK

You rub your hand on your sleeve and exclaim that your hand is now magnetized. To prove it to your audience, you grab hold of a metal spoon, let go of it, and the spoon magically clings to your hand. This is a fun trick that demonstrates **suspension**: when the magician is able to make something stay in the air and not fall.

HOW DO YOU DO IT?

If you were to really let go of the spoon, it would fall to the ground. But the audience doesn't know that you are secretly holding the spoon with the index finger of your other hand.

WHAT YOU NEED

• A spoon, fork, or any small, thin object such as a pencil or stick.

STEP 1

Grasp the spoon in your right hand. Use your left hand to grasp your right wrist. Be sure you keep your thumb on top and your fingers below.

STEP 2

Swing your body to the left and as you do, you extend your left forefinger out and press on the handle of the spoon in your fist and keep the right fingers closed.

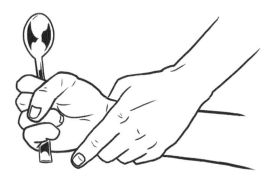

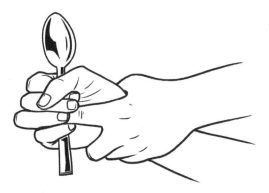

This is the view from your angle. The audience doesn't see this.

STEP 3

Now you slowly open up your right hand by extending the fingers. The illusion is that the spoon clings to your hand. Practice is required so that you can confidently hold the spoon with your left finger and keep the back of your hand toward the audience. You can even shake your hand up and down and show the spoon won't fall to the floor.

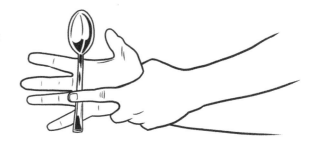

This is what you see.

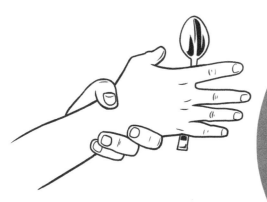

This is what the audience sees. Be sure to keep the back of your hand toward the audience.

Remember:
Practice this one in front of a mirror. This way you can see what the audience will see. When you do the secret move, be sure to swing your arms and body around and move your finger onto the spoon in one swift motion. Practice this until you can do it smoothly.

IT'S SHOWTIME!

Show both hands, front and back, to the audience. Have them check your hands to ensure there is no glue or tape stuck to them.

Tell the audience, "I will now turn my hand into a magnet. May I use your shirt sleeve please?" When they say yes, say, "Thank you. This will only take a second."

Reach over and rub the palm of your hand back and forth on their sleeve a few times. Look at your audience and exclaim, "My hand is now magnetized! I will prove it."

Now, pick the spoon up off your magic table and grip it in your right hand just like you did in practice. Grab your wrist with the left hand. Remember, the thumb goes on top, fingers below.

Swing your body and hands to the left so the back of hand is toward the spectator.

Now, slowly straighten your right fingers and say, **"Voila!"**

Tell the audience that you can release the magnetism. Look at the spoon and gently blow on it, and at the same time release the hold on the spoon by lifting your left finger off the spoon. The spoon will fall to the floor. Show your hands again to the audience. Take your bow and say, "Thank you."

☆ JACK THE JOLLY JUMPING RUBBER BAND ☆

Rubber Band Magic

THE TRICK

Before the audience can say "Abracadabra," a rubber band wrapped around your first and second fingers miraculously jumps to your third and fourth fingers.

HOW DO YOU DO IT?

The secret is how you wrap the rubber band around your fingers. This one takes some practice but is well worth it. In magic, this effect is known as a **transposition**: when a magician makes an object move from one place to another.

Parents: Find smaller rubber bands for your younger child's hand, about 1 inch in diameter. You can purchase a package of colored bands in various sizes at the dollar store or office supply store. You can also take a large band and tie a knot, thus making for a smaller loop. Assist them with this one as the bands will sometimes roll off the fingers accidentally.

WHAT YOU NEED

• A rubber band. Experiment with different sizes, depending on the size of your hand.

PRACTICE TIME

STEP 1

Hold one hand up with the palm facing you. Slip the band over the first two fingers. With your other hand, grasp the band and stretch it toward you.

STEP 2

Now close your first hand in a loose fist and as you do, stretch the band over the fingertips so the rubber band is now resting on the fingernails.

This is the side you don't show the audience.

STEP 3

Now rotate your hand so the audience only sees the back of your hand.

This is what the audience sees.

STEP 4

Pretend that your fingers are stuck together and won't separate. This will help you do the next part easily. Move your hand around in a giant circle and at the same time open your hand, making sure all four fingers move together, then close the hand to make a fist again. If you do this correctly, the rubber band will end up around the third and fourth fingers. Moving your hand around in a circle hides the secret move of you opening and closing your hand.

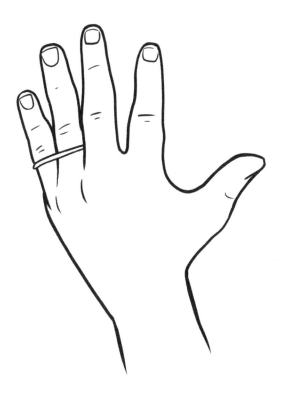

"Jack will perform an amazing feat of skill. He will jump over to the other two fingers."

Quickly move your hand in a large circle in front of your body. Ask the audience to say "jump" on the count of three.

"One . . . Two . . . Three . . . Jump!" (Do the secret move.) Slowly bring your hand to a rest. Show that Jack the Jolly Jumping Rubber Band has jumped over to the other two fingers as promised. Then say, "Everyone, please give Jack a round of applause."

IT'S SHOWTIME!

"And now, ladies and gentlemen, boys and girls," you say as you introduce your next feat of magic, "Say hello to Jack the Jolly Jumping Rubber Band."

Hold up the rubber band, and display it to the audience.

Place it on the first two fingers as you did in practice. Do the secret move you learned earlier, stretching it over the fingertips. Display the rubber band, showing that it is on the first two fingers.

TRY THIS

You can do a slightly harder version of this trick using two rubber bands: Jack and Jill—the Dynamic Duo. The Dynamic Duo jump across your fingers, changing places.

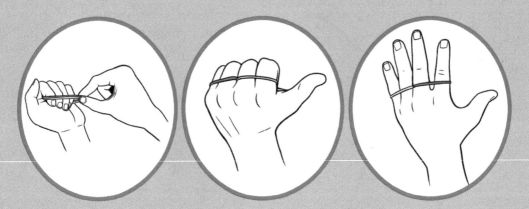

Get two different colored rubber bands. For example, one red and one yellow rubber band. Follow steps 1 through 3 as before, but this time put a red rubber band on your first two fingers and a yellow rubber band on your third and fourth fingers. Grasp both bands together and stretch them both over the fingertips.

Introduce the Dynamic Duo to your audience. "And now I am proud to introduce, Jack and Jill—the Dynamic Duo. Together they'll display their amazing talents by changing places in the blink of an eye." Always remember, your magic should be fun and engaging with interesting **patter**. Give your rubber bands some personality. Here I called them Jack and Jill. What names would you like to call them? I created a story about two performers doing feats of athleticism. Make up your own story.

Now open and close your hand. Say, "Ta-da!" as the audience sees that they have changed places. Pretty neat trick, huh?

☆ CAUGHT RED-HANDED ☆

I've Got Eyes in the Back of My Head

THE TRICK

You claim to have eyes in the back of your head and can tell which hand your friend is holding up in the air.

HOW DO YOU DO IT?

The secret is looking at your friend's hands to see which one is lighter in color than the other.

WHAT YOU NEED

- Any objects that you can hold in your hands will do. Here we will use a spoon and a fork from the dinner table. You can also use a dime and a penny, or a pencil and ruler.

PRACTICE TIME
STEP 1
Hold the fork in one hand and the spoon in the other hand. Put one hand up high in the air as shown here.

STEP 2
Slowly count to 10. As you are counting, what do you notice? Your hand starts getting tired because the blood in your hand is moving down your arm.

STEP 3
Now, hold both hands out in front of you with your palms up so you can see the underside of your wrists. Look at the color of your skin. Do you notice something? The underside of the hand that was held up will be a little bit lighter than the hand that was down at your side because there is now less blood in it.

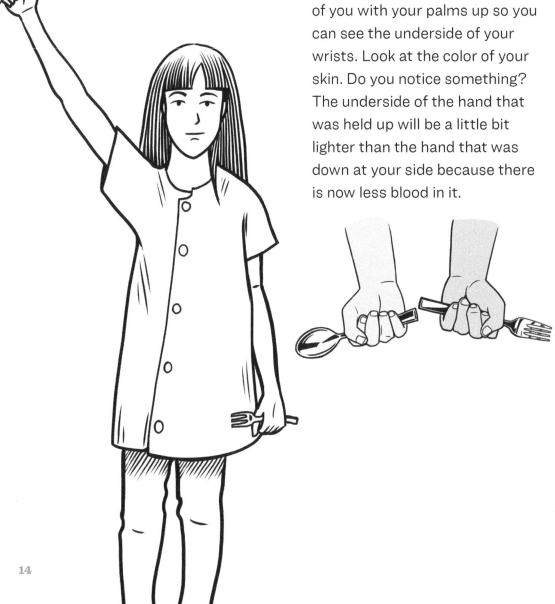

IT'S SHOWTIME!

Stand next to your magic table, and place a spoon and fork on top. Say, "I need the assistance of someone in the audience." Look for the person who is smiling and eager to help out.

"Please come up. Let's give them a round of applause."

Say, "After I turn my back to you, I will give you some instructions. Are you ready?" When they say yes, turn around so your back is to your helper.

Say, "Okay, now pick up the spoon and fork. Hold one in each hand." When they say that they have done it, tell them, "Hold one object high in the air above your head and keep holding it up." You can demonstrate this by putting one hand up in the air and the other hand down by your side.

"I will count to 10, and when I reach 10 put both hands out in front of your body."

Here you stall for time, so their hand begins to get tired. Tell them you have eyes in the back of your head just like your parents say they do. Of course, your friend will find that funny.

After you reach 10, instruct your friend to hold both hands out in front of them, palms up. You can demonstrate by showing them with your hands.

Turn around. Look quickly at their hands and notice which hand is lighter in color. Now, look into their eyes and say, "Hmm, the eyes in the back of my head are telling me you were holding the spoon up in the air." Here you name the object that's in the hand that is lighter in color.

☆ LINKING PAPER CLIPS ☆

Solid Passes through Solid

THE TRICK

Two paper clips become linked together. This is an example of what magicians call **penetration**: when one solid object appears to pass through another solid object.

HOW DO YOU DO IT?

By magic, of course! And with the help of a dollar bill.

WHAT YOU NEED

- Two paper clips. Try to find large paper clips—they are easier to work with.
- A dollar bill, or a rectangular piece of paper that's 2 inches wide by 6 inches long

PRACTICE TIME

First, let's look at the paper clip and understand how they are used. See the two rounded ends? Pull back on the longest rounded end and slide that onto the dollar bill. The bill will be clipped between the two sections. Now, let's learn how to fold the dollar bill and put the paper clips on.

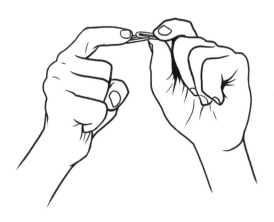

STEP 1

It will help to study the illustrations. Fold one end of the paper over as shown here. Place the paper clip onto the bill as shown.

STEP 2

Now, fold the other end of the bill around the back of the bill and be sure it extends out.

Place the paper clip on this section. If you did this correctly, you will see only one clip on each side. The two ends of the dollar bill will become handles for you to hold.

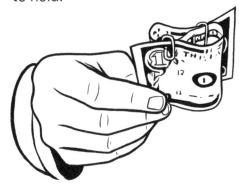

STEP 3

Now grasp the corners of the bill as in the illustration. Pull the ends apart, and as you do, you will see the clips move together. Keep pulling, and the clips will pass around each other and fly off the bill. Pick up one clip and—voila! You just linked them together.

Have fun getting the two clips apart! With practice you'll have them apart in no time. Now practice again until it becomes a "piece of cake."

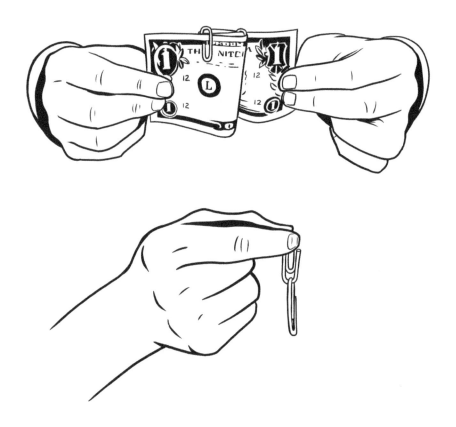

IT'S SHOWTIME!

Ask to borrow a dollar bill from the audience—if they don't have one, you can use a rectangular piece of paper (have one handy in your **magic box**—see page 124). Hold up the paper clips and show them to the audience.

Announce that this is a story of two kids who lived on a winding street. As you say that, fold the bill into the shape of an *S*. Pick up one clip and say, "This is Peter. He lived on one end of the street." As you say this, place the clip on the paper as you practiced in step 1.

Now, pick up the second clip and say, "This is Sally. She lived on the other end of the street."

Place the clip on the paper as you did in step 2.

Say, "Sally and Peter were friends forever. They both went off to college, and when they came home, they fell in love." Tell your audience to all say, "Ahh, how sweet!"

Pull on the ends of the paper, then pick the clips up and show they are now linked. "Then, they got married and lived happily ever after."

Feel free to make up your own story here that suits you. The audience will enjoy hearing you tell a story you made up.

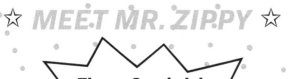

☆ MEET MR. ZIPPY ☆

Zipper Sandwich Bag Magic

THE TRICK

The zipper opening of a plastic sandwich bag magically bends forward and backward at your command.

HOW DO YOU DO IT?

You are secretly sliding the two sides of the zipper with your thumb and fingers, causing the plastic to bend. This effect in magic is known as **animation**.

WHAT YOU NEED

- A sandwich bag with a zipper
- A pair of scissors
- A ruler

MAKING THE PROPS

Cut off the bottom part of the bag just below the zipper opening. Use the ruler as a guide to help you cut a straight line. Be sure to recycle the lower part you cut off. Finally, snip off one end of the zipper.

PRACTICE TIME
STEP 1

Hold the plastic zipper in your right hand between your thumb and fingers at the end that was cut off. By pushing up with your thumb, you can make the plastic bend forward, away from you.

Don't forget to hold the zipper at the end that you snipped off.

STEP 2

Now pull down with your thumb, and the plastic moves backward, toward you.

Practice these secret moves several times, and do it slowly so your audience doesn't see you moving your thumb and fingers.

IT'S SHOWTIME!

Hold the plastic strip up in your right hand, look at the audience, and say, "Please meet my friend, Mr. Zippy. Take a bow, Mr. Zippy." Do the secret move you practiced and make the plastic bend forward, then slowly bend it back to its upright position.

With a big smile, say, "I will now hypnotize Mr. Zippy." Wave your left hand around in a circle above Mr. Zippy. "Sleep!" As you say this, bend the plastic backward.

"Mr. Zippy is now in a deep sleep." Look at the audience, and put your left finger to your lips and say, "Shh, quiet, he's sleeping."

"Now I will wake him up. Mr. Zippy, wake up!" Here you bend the plastic back to its upright position.

Say, "Now, Mr. Zippy will do some simple math. Mr. Zippy, what is 1 + 1?"

Bend the plastic forward two times and count as you do, saying, "One, two."

Look surprised and say, "That's right. Very good."

Say, "Okay, what is 2 x 2?" Bend the plastic forward again, four times. Get the audience to cheer every time Mr. Zippy is right.

"Now, Mr. Zippy will dance for us." Start to hum a tune with your voice, and make Mr. Zippy bend forward then backward and forward again. "Look at him dance!"

End the trick by telling your audience that Mr. Zippy is tired and will say goodbye now. Say, "Thank you, Mr. Zippy." Tell your audience to clap for Mr. Zippy and have it bow forward again.

TRY THIS

Draw eyes, a nose, and a mouth on a piece of paper. Cut them out and tape them to the plastic strip on the top side (that hasn't been cut). Now your Mr. Zippy has a face! Or, draw a flower and a sun. Cut them each out and tape the flower to the plastic strip on the uncut side. Show the flower to the audience in one hand, and hold the sun in your other hand. Pass the sun over the flower from side to side, and at the same time bend the flower so it follows the sun.

This is a great trick for you to create your own story. Don't forget to make it fun, and be a little silly, too.

The Appearing Knot

THE TRICK

Holding a length of rope in your hand, you give it a shake and a knot magically appears.

HOW DO YOU DO IT?

There is already a knot in the rope, but your audience is none the wiser because you are hiding the knot in your hand.

WHAT YOU NEED

• A length of rope, about 18 to 24 inches long

PRACTICE TIME
STEP 1
Start by tying a single knot in the rope about 6 inches from one end.

STEP 2
Hold the rope in the right hand. Close your hand around the knot so the audience does not see it.

STEP 3
Grab hold of the rope at the bottom end with the left hand and bring it up to the top, then transfer it to the thumb and first finger in your right hand.

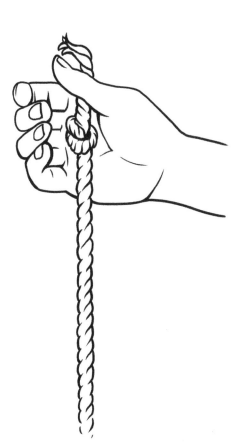

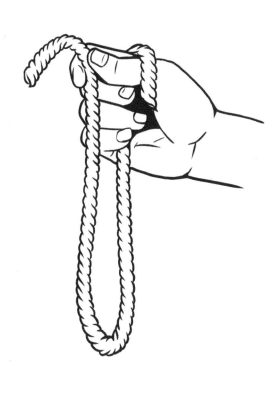

STEP 4

Give the rope a good shake with your right hand two times. On the second shake, open your hand and let the end with the knot fall. Be sure to keep holding the other end with the thumb and finger. What you have done is turn the rope upside down. Now the knot is at the bottom of the rope.

STEP 5

The illusion is perfect. It appears that by shaking the rope, a knot magically appears. Point to the knot and say, "Ta-da!" Be sure to close the right hand into a fist so it looks the same as when you started.

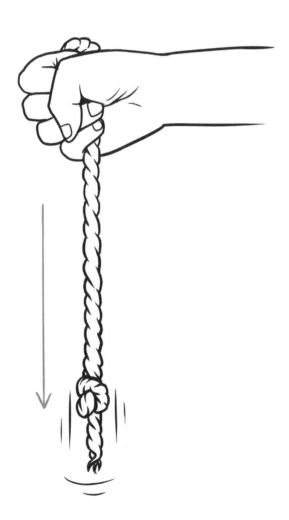

IT'S SHOWTIME!

Have the rope in your magic box with the knot tied at one end, ready to perform.

Say, "Now it's time for some rope magic!" Pick up the rope from your magic box and hold it up for your audience to see.

Point to the rope and say, "I will make a knot magically appear."

Shake the rope two times, but don't switch ends. Act like the trick worked, smile, and say, "Ta-da!"

Look at the rope and notice there is no knot. Look surprised and say, "Oh yeah, we forgot to say the magic words."

Now, bring the end back up and grip it again with the thumb and finger.

Tell your audience to say the magic words, "Abra-Rope-Dabra."

Give the rope two good shakes again, and this time you secretly switch the ends. Your audience will gasp when they see the knot appear.

When the knot appears, point to it with your left hand and say, "Ta-da!" Hand out the rope for examination if you like.

INTERMEDIATE TRICKS

☆ VEGETABLE MAGIC ☆

Transform a Carrot into Celery

THE TRICK

You roll a carrot up in a napkin. After saying the magic words, the napkin is unrolled and the carrot **transforms** into celery.

HOW DO YOU DO IT?

The celery is hidden under the napkin. When rolling up the napkin, you secretly **switch** the two vegetables.

WHAT YOU NEED

- A cloth napkin or bandana
- 1 carrot
- 1 stalk of celery (other similarly shaped vegetables or objects will work, too!)

PRACTICE TIME
STEP 1

Place the celery on the table and cover it with the cloth napkin. Be sure the napkin is oriented as shown. You want to put a few creases in the napkin to hide the celery underneath.

STEP 2

Now place the carrot down on top of the napkin just above the celery.

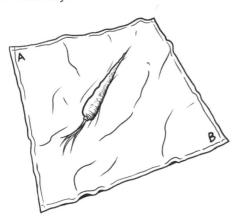

STEP 4

Keep rolling until the top corner (A) and bottom corner (B) reach the center.

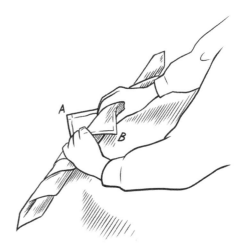

STEP 3

Now grasp both the carrot and the celery and start rolling the napkin up.

When the corners are at the center, turn the napkin over.

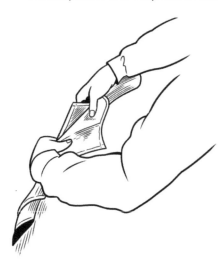

STEP 6

Ta-da! The celery will be on top and the carrot will be underneath.

STEP 5

Say the magic words, "Vegetable Magic!" Now you grasp the corners at A and B with your hands apart, unrolling the napkin.

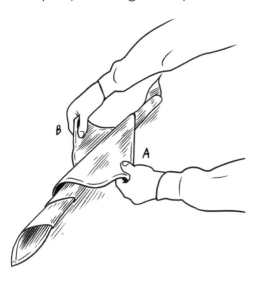

IT'S SHOWTIME!

You need to set this up ahead of time before anyone is in the room. Put the celery on the kitchen table and cover it with the napkin.

Ask family members to come into the room and see your vegetable magic trick.

Bring out the carrot and say, "Do you know what's inside this carrot?"

They will, of course, say no. You reply, "Inside this carrot is vitamin A."

They will be impressed that you know this.

Say, "Now, I will do something amazing with this carrot." Place the carrot on the napkin as you did in practice. Start rolling up the napkin.

When you get to the point where you are about to turn the napkin over, look up at your audience, make eye contact, and ask them to say the magic words, "Vegetable Magic!" When they say that, quickly turn the napkin over.

Now unwrap the napkin and see the expression on their faces when they see the piece of celery.

Hand out the celery for examination. Casually pick up the carrot and napkin together and put them away in your box.

For an added laugh, bring out a salt shaker from your magic box, sprinkle salt on the celery, and take a bite. Smile and say, "Yum! That's refreshing!"

Magic at Your Fingertips

THE TRICK

You make a straw instantly **vanish** and then appear at your fingertips.

HOW DO YOU DO IT?

The straw is secretly taped to your thumb and becomes cleverly hidden from the audience's view.

WHAT YOU NEED

- A paper or plastic drinking straw—cut to about 4 to 6 inches in length (experiment with the length depending on the size of your hand)
- Clear sticky tape

PRACTICE TIME
STEP 1
Make a loop of tape by rolling it around and press it on your thumbnail. Now press the straw on the tape so it stays.

STEP 2
Practice these moves in front of a mirror so you can see how it looks. With the straw taped to your thumb, bend your thumb in and hold the straw in a fist between your thumb and your first finger.

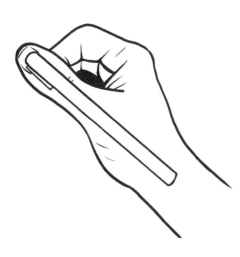

STEP 3
Now open your hand quickly, and amazingly, the straw appears to vanish. Of course, it's hidden behind your hand. Look in the mirror and watch the angles. Position your hand so the straw won't be seen by the audience.

STEP 4

Now to make the straw reappear! Close your hand back to the position where you started.

Use your other hand as misdirection and to add drama.

IT'S SHOWTIME!

This is one of those quick tricks you can do in the middle of your show or if someone asks you to show them something quick.

Away from the audience's view, put the tape on your thumb and push the straw onto the tape.

Tell the audience, "Please watch closely."

Now, bring your hand out (with the straw secretly taped to your thumb) and show the straw to the audience, holding it the way you practiced in step 2. Ask them to say, "Go!" Now open your hand and say, "It's gone."

Look around in front of you. Pretend you see the straw floating in the air. Now pause for a moment, and say, "There it is!"

Reach out with your hand, then close your fist to make it reappear. The illusion you created is as if you pulled the straw out of the air.

TRY THIS

Get a second straw and stick it to your other thumb. Practice making one disappear and then the other appear. Create the **illusion** that one straw is jumping from one hand to the other and back again.

☆ LEVITATING LATTE ☆

Floating Coffee Cup

WHAT IT LOOKS LIKE

In this quick trick, you appear to mysteriously **levitate** a coffee cup.

HOW IT'S DONE

You never let go of the cup completely. The audience can't see that you are really holding it with your thumb.

WHAT YOU NEED

- A paper drinking cup

MAKING THE PROP

Find a paper cup from a café or restaurant or ask your family for a disposable cup they are about to recycle. Wash it out and then very carefully puncture a hole in the back of the cup with the handle of a fork or spoon. The hole must be large enough for your thumb to fit snugly, so the cup will stay on tightly and not fall off.

PRACTICE TIME

You will want to practice this in front of a mirror so you can see what the audience sees.

STEP 1

Push either your left or right thumb into the hole you made. Be sure that the cup fits snugly and does not fall off. Now, grip the sides of the cup with the fingers of both hands.

STEP 2

Now to create the illusion that the cup is floating, slowly lift your fingers off the cup so that the cup is held only by your thumb. Wiggle your fingers to create some mystery.

STEP 3

To make the cup appear to be floating away from you, slowly move your hands forward, extending your arms. When the cup has floated away about 6 to 12 inches, stop moving and grab the cup with your fingers as if you are catching it. Now, return the cup back to the starting position by pulling it toward you.

STEP 4

When you finish, take your thumb out and pull the cup away.

IT'S SHOWTIME!

Say, "And now it's time for the latte levitation." Bring out the coffee cup, holding it in both hands. Slip your thumb into the hole.

Say, "Don't blink. Something mysterious is about to happen." Wait a few seconds for the suspense to build.

Ask your audience to say the magic words, "Latte Magic!" Make an eerie sound with your voice. You can even whistle if you know how. Remove your fingers from the cup, and show the cup is levitating.

Say, "Wait, there's more." Now make the cup float away from you, then back toward you. Then the cup slowly floats up and then back down.

Say, "Okay, that's enough coffee for the day." Return the cup to the starting position. Grip it with your fingers.

This is a fun and quick little trick to do. It's a perfect trick to do in the middle of your magic show.

TRY THIS

You will need two cups in your **magic box** (see page 124). One cup does not have a hole. The other cup has the hole you punch for your thumb. You will also need a bandana or small scarf.

Say, "And now it's time for the latte levitation." Pass out the unprepared cup.

Say, "Please examine this cup." After the cup has been examined, take it back and reach into your magic box to take out the bandana—at the same time, **switch** the cups so you end up holding the cup with the hole in it. Be sure the audience does not see the hole.

Say, "And please examine this scarf." While they are examining the scarf, put your thumb into the hole and hold the cup with the fingers of that hand.

Say, "I don't have a latte to put in this cup, so I'll use this bandana." Take the bandana back and put it into the cup. And now hold the cup with the other hand.

Now, do the floating illusion as you learned earlier.

When the cup returns to the starting position, remove the bandana, wipe the cup out, put it away, and say, "Okay, that's enough coffee for the day."

☆ MULTIPLYING MONEY I ☆

I Can Make Money, and I Don't Even Have a Job!

THE TRICK

You pour some coins (13 cents) from a bowl into your friend's hand. When they count the coins, they find the money has suddenly doubled (26 cents).

HOW DO YOU DO IT?

There is a secret pocket under the bowl holding the extra coins.

WHAT YOU NEED

- A shallow bowl or saucer plate. It should be no more than 6 inches in diameter.
- A piece of light cardboard or cardstock, measuring 4 inches long by 2½ inches wide
- Some coins: six pennies and four nickels
- Scissors
- Clear tape

MAKING THE PROPS
STEP 1
Fold the cardboard strip into thirds, overlapping the edges.

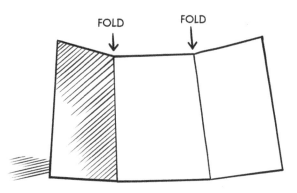

STEP 2
Tape down the edges. Then fold one of the open ends over and tape it down. You now have a small pocket to hold a few coins inside.

STEP 3
Tape the pocket you made to the bottom of a shallow bowl or small plate saucer.

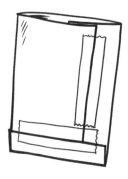

STEP 4
Put three pennies and two nickels inside this secret pocket and set the bowl on the table.

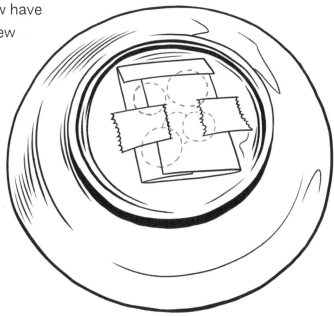

PRACTICE TIME
STEP 1
Put the rest of the coins inside the bowl. Be careful the coins in the secret pocket don't fall out.

STEP 2
Hold the bowl in your right hand. Be sure the opening to the secret pocket is facing to your left.

STEP 3
Hold your left palm out, tip the bowl letting the coins fall into your palm, and at the same time allow the coins in the pocket to fall with the other coins. As soon as the coins fall into your hand, close your left hand into a fist.

(Note: Remember to hold the bowl on the opposite side of the opening to the pocket.)

STEP 4
Say the magic words, "Show me the money!" Now open your hand. VOILA! You have just doubled your money!

Load the two nickels and three pennies back into the secret pocket, and put the rest of the coins in the bowl and practice again. Remember to keep track

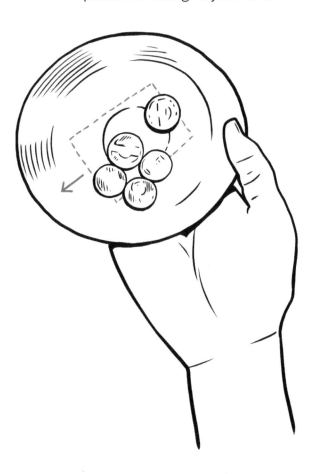

of which way the opening to the pocket is so you can pick up the bowl the correct way. Practice this several times until you can do it smoothly.

IT'S SHOWTIME!

Say to the audience, "Hey, I know how to make money, and I don't even have a job!"

With your right hand, pick up the bowl from your magic table.

Ask the audience, "How much money do I have here?"

Of course, they will say, "13 cents."

You say, "I'll show you how I can double my money."

Pour the money out into your hand as you did in practice (the coins in the pocket will fall out, too). Close your hand immediately into a fist. Hold your fist up in the air. Shake the coins a few times.

Tell everybody to say, "Show me the money!"

Open your hand and say "Voila! I just doubled my money."

Ask them to count the change. Expect the audience to say, "Wow, how did you do that?"

Smile at them and say, "Very well, thank you."

TRY THIS

What can you use instead of a bowl? Try a saucer plate. How about a drink coaster? Ask your parents to borrow a drink coaster, and tape your piece of cardboard to the bottom of it. Place the coins inside this pocket and put the rest of the coins on top.

Experiment with different coins. Try doing this with quarters and dimes.

☆ MULTIPLYING MONEY II ☆

Sleight of Hand with Coins

THE TRICK

A penny at your fingertips magically changes into two quarters. This is a good example of **close-up** magic, which are tricks that are done in close range of a small group of people.

HOW DO YOU DO IT?

The quarters are secretly hidden behind the penny.

WHAT YOU NEED

- Two large coins, such as two quarters or half-dollars
- A small coin, such as a penny or a dime

This trick is a good one to learn about **sleight of hand**. Practice this in front of a mirror. Watch your angles—the audience should not be able to see the quarters hiding behind the penny.

PRACTICE TIME
STEP 1
Begin by stacking the two quarters together and holding the edge of the coins between your thumb and first finger.

STEP 2
Now place the penny in front of the coins with the head facing the audience and pinch it with your thumb and first finger. The coins will join perpendicularly: the edges of the quarters should be touching the tail side of the penny, like so.

STEP 3
Showing that your other hand is empty, reach over and slide the penny underneath the quarters with your thumb.

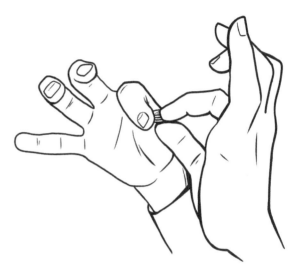

STEP 4
Bring the hand forward and turn the stack so the quarters are facing the audience. Now, split the stack of quarters, taking a quarter in each hand. The penny will be hidden from view behind one of the quarters.

You can end here or you can do another secret move and ditch the penny, getting rid of it without anyone knowing.

To ditch the penny, let the coin that doesn't have the penny behind it fall into your palm. Then start to place the other coin on top of the coin in your palm, but as you do, slide the penny back with your thumb and keep it hidden in your hand. Hand the two coins out for examination. Go to your magic box to get rid of the penny. Pick up whatever you need to start your next trick.

IT'S SHOWTIME!

When no one is watching or inside your magic box, stack the two quarters and pinch the penny in front. Then come out and hold your hand up like you did in practice. Point to the penny with your

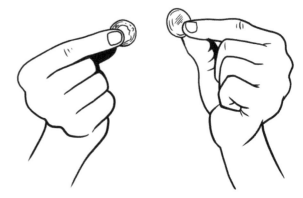

other hand and say, "Don't blink, because something magical is about to happen at my fingertips."

Ask the audience to say the magic words, "Show me the money!" As they say it, do the secret move to turn the penny into two quarters, and split them, holding one in each hand.

End by putting the two quarters in your pocket (or in your magic box) along with the penny and say, "Two quarters. That's it!"

☆ DON'T CRY, GEORGE! ☆

Squeeze a Quarter, Make It Cry Tears

THE TRICK

You pretend to squeeze a quarter so hard that it begins to cry tears and waterdrops appear.

HOW DO YOU DO IT?

George isn't a crybaby, but you can make it appear he is. You are secretly holding a small wad of wet paper behind the quarter. When you squeeze the quarter, water appears.

WHAT YOU NEED

- A quarter is the best size coin to use. A half-dollar or a dollar coin will also work.
- A paper towel, paper napkin, or tissue
- A glass of water

PRACTICE TIME
STEP 1

Tear off a small piece from the paper napkin, about 2 inches square.

Now wad the napkin into a tiny ball. Soak the napkin in the water. Squeeze out a little water so it's not dripping wet.

STEP 2

Have the coin in your pocket or in your magic box. Hiding the wet paper ball in your right hand, pick up the coin with the left hand and hold it at your fingertips.

STEP 3

Now, secretly add the wet paper ball onto the back of the coin and as you do, hold the right side of the coin with your right fingertips. You are now holding the coin at the tip of your fingers with the wet ball behind. Hold the ball with your thumbs in back and your fingers in front of the coin. This secret move is what magicians call **sleight of hand**.

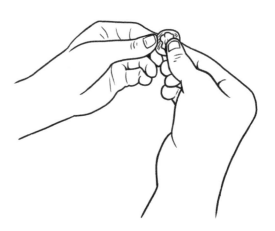

STEP 4

Now, start to squeeze the quarter. Make a grimace with your face as if you are squeezing really hard. At the same time, press your thumbs against the wet ball.

STEP 5

Water will drip down. Wet the ball and practice again.

The right hand has been removed for clarity.

IT'S SHOWTIME!

Before you perform this trick, be sure you have the wet paper ball in your magic box or behind your magic table. Now you can easily pick up the ball, hiding it in your right hand, then reach in your pocket to remove the coin (we will assume it's a quarter). Ask someone, "Who is the president on the quarter?" They will say, "George Washington."

Tell them, "Did you know that George is a crybaby?"

Show the coin to your audience so they can see George on the front.

"Because when I squeeze the coin, George feels it and will start to cry. Here, I will show you."

Ask someone to hold out their hand, palm up, underneath the coin.

Start to squeeze the coin as you did in practice. Secretly press the wet ball with your thumbs. Let them see the water start to drip.

Have them remove their hand and look at the water.

Take the coin with your left hand and place it in their palm. As you do this, secretly put your right hand in your pocket and ditch the wet ball. Or you can put your hand in your magic box and leave the ball there.

Conclude your act by saying, "Oh, poor George. He's such a crybaby!"

☆ COIN IN ELBOW ☆

Make a Coin Vanish Then Reappear

THE TRICK

The magician rubs a quarter in their elbow, and it disappears and reappears in their pocket.

HOW DO YOU DO IT?

Using **sleight of hand**, the quarter is secretly transferred to the other hand.

WHAT YOU NEED

• A quarter or coin that is large enough to fit in your hand

This one requires some easy sleight of hand and good acting. Practice this until you can do it with confidence.

PRACTICE TIME
STEP 1
Hold the coin in the palm of your right hand. Hold up your left elbow and place your left hand on your neck.

STEP 2
Place the coin against the elbow and make a rubbing motion.

STEP 3

Now let the coin fall out of your right hand and land on the ground. Reach down with BOTH hands to pick up the coin.

STEP 4

Pick up the coin with your right hand. Stand up and rub the coin into your elbow again. Then, let the coin slip out of your hand and fall to the ground again.

Now here comes the secret move. Reach down with both hands again to retrieve the coin, but this time pick up the coin in your right hand and secretly transfer the coin into the left hand and immediately close it into a fist. No one should see you put the coin in the other hand.

Tip:
Act like you didn't mean to drop the coin—this will keep the audience off guard for when you do the secret move.

STEP 5

Now stand back up and hold your right hand as if the coin is there, and start rubbing your right hand into your elbow just like the last time. The audience will think the coin is still in your right hand. Good acting is important here to make them believe the coin is still there.

Blow on your elbow and slowly take your right hand away and show the coin is gone. Wait for the audience to realize what happened. Then reach into your left pocket as if the coin is really there and come out showing the coin.

IT'S SHOWTIME!

Say, "I've got something cool to show you with a coin."

Start rubbing the coin in your elbow and let it fall to the ground. Say, "Oops, let me try that again."

Pick up coin, rub again, and let the coin fall to the ground a second time. Say, "Oops, I've got the dropsies today!"

Do the secret move, picking up the coin in the right hand, then switching the coin to the left hand. Rub a third time. Stop rubbing and say, "Here's the cool part. All I have to do is blow on my elbow and . . ."

Slowly open your right hand to show it's empty and finish your line by saying, ". . . the coin vanishes."

Say, "You may be wondering where it went." Reach in your pocket with the coin still hidden in your left hand. Then bring it out and show it. Say, "Here it is."

TRY THIS

When you rub the final time in step 5, place the coin in your left hand onto the back of your neck and let it stay there (this takes some practice—the key is to keep your head still so the coin doesn't slide off). Finish rubbing and show that your hands are empty.

Then point to your elbow and say, "The coin has passed through my skin and into my arm. It's traveling up my arm, across my chest, and around my neck, and it will come out here at the back of my neck." As you say the last line, reach up with your right hand, pick up the coin, and hold it up for everyone to see.

(Right hand reaches up to remove coin left there when you were rubbing your elbow.)

☆ COLOR VISION ☆

Mind-Reading Magic

THE TRICK

A volunteer hands you a crayon behind your back. You then become a **mentalist** and read their mind, telling them the color of the crayon.

HOW DO YOU DO IT?

You don't really read their mind—that would be cool if you could. You secretly rub the crayon on your thumbnail and take a sneak peek at the color.

WHAT YOU NEED

- A few crayons. I suggest you get three to five crayons, including colors such as red, blue, orange, purple, and green. Some crayons work better than others. Avoid light colors or similar colors because you may not be able to see them or tell the difference.
- A small box or envelope to hold the crayons

PRACTICE TIME
STEP 1

Let's practice this first so we can perform it with confidence. Put the crayons you've selected into a box and set the box down on a table. Turn around and with both hands behind your back, pick up one crayon out of the box. You don't know what color it is, so no peeking!

STEP 2

With your hands still behind your back, draw (or scratch) some of the crayon on your thumbnail. You have to press hard enough to get the waxy crayon to come off. When you're done, put the crayon back into the box. You have no idea what color the crayon is, now do you? Here's the secret method.

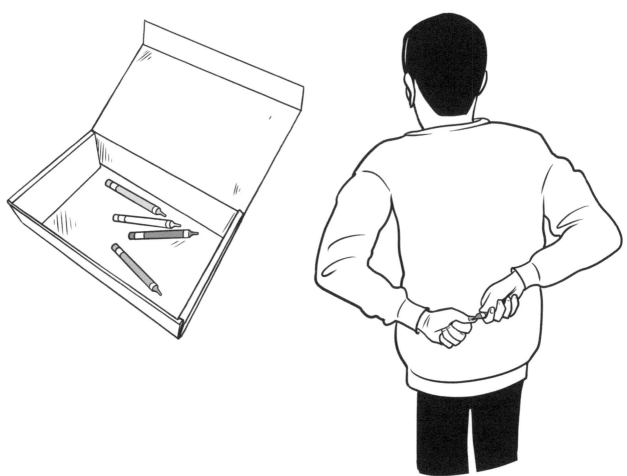

STEP 3

Bring the hand with the crayon mark on it around in front and extend it out. Look straight ahead across the room and take a quick peek at the crayon on your thumbnail. Now you know the color. No one knows you have marked your thumbnail.

Here you are looking straight ahead, while at the same time getting a quick glance at your thumbnail.

STEP 4

Scratch the crayon off on your thumbnail and practice steps 1 through 3 again with a different color. Practice this until you can do it with confidence.

IT'S SHOWTIME!

Begin by saying, "And now, a demonstration of mind-reading. Who would like to volunteer?" Have your volunteer come up with a round of applause.

Place the box of crayons on the table in front of your volunteer and say, "Please think of one of these colors."

Now turn your back to them. Say, "Hand me the color you are thinking of, and then close the lid on the box."

After your volunteer has handed you the crayon and closed the box, turn back around and tell them to look into your eyes. As you stare into their eyes, this is when you do the secret move of rubbing some crayon on your thumbnail.

When you have done the secret move, bring the hand out

from behind your back, and hold it up high in front of the volunteer's eyes. Make a mysterious motion by moving your hand around in a circle. Now stare into your volunteer's eyes and say, "Look into my eyes."

Say, "I see a color. One color brighter than all the others. I see the color . . . red!" Here you announce the color that is on your thumbnail.

Bring the crayon out from behind your back and say, "I was right!" Then look at them with a grin and say, "Don't tell anyone, but I have eyes in the back of my head!"

TRY THIS

Instead of using a box with a lid, you could put the crayons in an envelope, or have your helper just hold the crayons in their hands. Be sure to tell them to hide the other crayons so you can't see them when you turn back around to read their mind.

This is a trick that you can repeat over again. And when you do, tell them that you can see the color in their eyes. If the color is similar to what they are wearing, then make a connection to the color of their clothes.

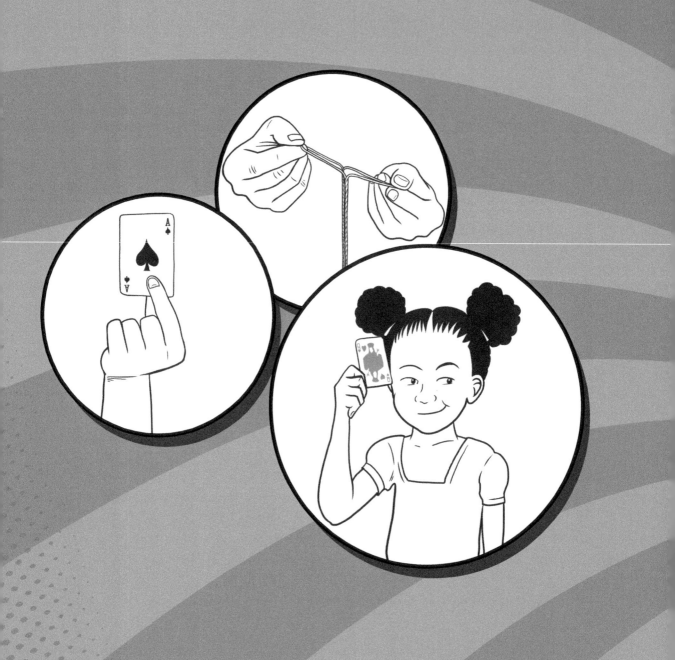

ADVANCED TRICKS

☆ AMAZING STRING TRICK ☆

Two Strings Melt into One

THE TRICK

Show two pieces of string to your audience. With a gentle pull, you are able to magically make the two pieces melt into one. Now that's magic!

HOW DO YOU DO IT?

The illusion is that you are holding two separate strings, but in reality, it's only one string that is made to look like two separate strings.

WHAT YOU NEED

- To perform this cool illusion, you will need a certain type of string that is composed of many individual strands twisted together. This type of string is referred to as twine. You can get this string at most grocery stores or the dollar store.
- Scissors

MAKING THE PROPS
STEP 1
Before you perform this, you must first prepare the string in a special way. Cut a piece of twine about 18 inches long. Locate the center of the string and spread the strands apart, separating them into two equal pieces.

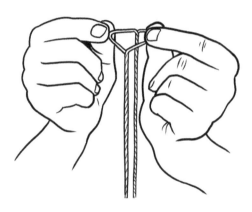

STEP 2
Pull on the two pieces about 2 inches. You can use the length of your thumb as a measuring guide.

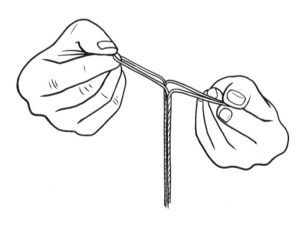

STEP 3
Now straighten out these pieces and twist them between your fingers so that they come together to form what appears to be the ends of the two strings.

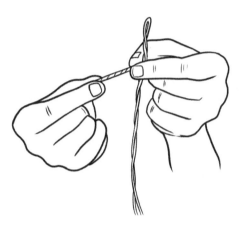

STEP 4
Put the string you've prepared in your magic box. You are now ready to perform this amazing trick.

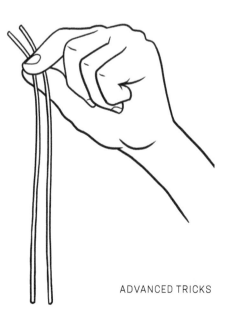

PRACTICE TIME

STEP 1

Pick up the string from your box and hold it with your thumb and first finger at the place where the pieces join.

STEP 3

Close your hand around the string. Don't make a tight fist. It should be loose enough for the string to be pulled.

STEP 2

Place your other hand in between the two strands, and lay the center on your palm.

STEP 4

Now slowly pull on the string at one end. Be careful that the center piece does not come out of your hand.

STEP 5

Now slowly pull on the opposite side. As you continue to pull, you will feel the string in your hand coming together.

When they have finally come together, stop pulling and make a rubbing motion with your hand.

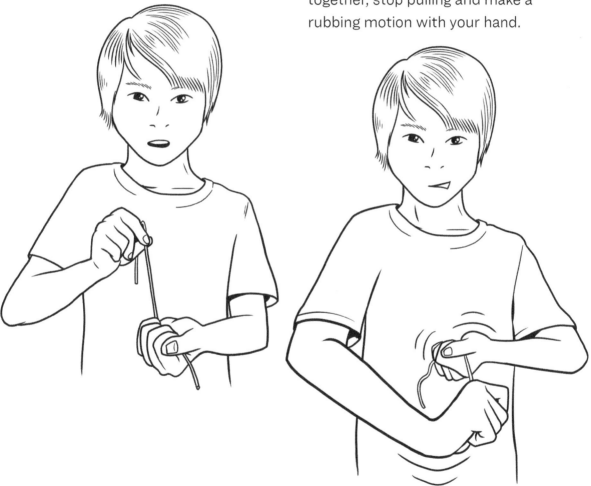

STEP 6

Now slowly open up your hand and show the two strings have magically become one.

IT'S SHOWTIME!

Be sure you have prepared the string ahead of time and have it ready to go in your magic box. Here you will have the spectator hold the ends and pull, unlike in practice where you were doing the pulling.

Pick up the string from your box and show it to the audience. Say something silly such as, "This is called the two-string trick. It's called the two-string trick because it uses two strings."

Now ask a spectator to grasp the real ends of the string. They will think that they are holding on to two separate strings. Tell them not to let go. Close your fist around the center. Make a gentle rubbing motion with your fingers.

Tell your helper to pull gently on the ends until you tell them to stop. (You will begin to feel the pieces coming together in your closed fist—that's when you tell them to stop pulling.) Now wave your other hand over your closed fist.

Say the magic words, "Two become one!" Now, slowly open your hand to show that the two strings have magically "melted" themselves together into one single piece. Tug on the string and show that it really is one piece of string. You can hand out the string for examination.

This is a wonderful **illusion** and will completely baffle your audience. Make a new piece of string when the first gets worn out.

TRY THIS

Once you have mastered this trick, here's another way of performing it that will really fool your audience. Have the prepared string in your magic box. Also have two single pieces, about 12 inches in length. To begin the trick, take out the two single strings and show them. Then, act as if you forgot something, and go back inside your box with the strings to remove a magic wand, and at the same time leave the two single pieces behind and bring out the prepared string. The audience will not notice that you secretly switched the strings.

☆ KITCHEN MAGICIAN ☆

Mind-Reading in the Kitchen

THE TRICK

Tell your assistant to come into the room and, after pointing to a few objects, your assistant instantly knows what object was selected by an audience volunteer.

HOW DO YOU DO IT?

You and your assistant use a secret code. After you point to a few objects, you then point to a black object and that tells your assistant that the next object will be the one the audience volunteer has chosen.

Tip: If the kitchen has lots of black objects, then you may want to decide on a different secret color.

WHAT YOU NEED

• Someone who can be your assistant

PRACTICE TIME

You will need to practice this with an assistant, so they understand the secret, too.

Read this over carefully so you understand it, then teach it to your assistant.

STEP 1

Ask a friend or family member to be your assistant.

STEP 2

Tell them that you will point to several objects in the kitchen, and you will ask them if another volunteer from the audience is thinking of that object. They should answer "no."

STEP 3

Have them pay close attention to the color of the objects. When you point to a black-colored object, that will be their clue. The next object you touch will be the object that the volunteer selected. Then they are to say, "Yes, that's the item you are thinking of."

IT'S SHOWTIME!

Invite a friend or a family member into the kitchen to serve as the audience. Tell them that you and your assistant are going to demonstrate mind-reading. Instruct your assistant to leave the kitchen so they cannot see or hear.

Now, tell the audience member to point to any object in the kitchen (another room in the house works fine, too). Tell them that it can be something on the wall, a kitchen appliance, a drawer or cabinet door, anything.

Now call for your assistant to return. Tell your assistant, "This audience member is thinking of an object." Now point to something that's not black—for example, the calendar.

Say, "Are they thinking of this calendar?" Your assistant will answer no.

Ask again, "Are they thinking of this towel?" They will say no again.

Ask again, "Are they thinking of the clock?" They will say no again.

Ask again, "Are they thinking of the light switch?" They will say no again.

Now, you point to a black object and say, "Are they thinking of the oven?" Your assistant will again say no. But that will give them the clue that the next object is the right one.

Now point to the object that the audience member has chosen and say to your assistant, "Are they thinking of this bottle?" They will say, "Yes!"

Congratulations! Take a bow! Your friend will be puzzled.

TRY THIS

You can even repeat this trick for the same audience but use a different color—like red for example. You and your assistant must decide in advance what color you will use as your clue for the second round.

Instruct the assistant to gaze into the helper's eyes with a puzzled look before finally saying, "Yes, that's the item." Or, have them say, "Let me look into your eyes . . . oh yes, I see now—you are thinking of the chair!" You can really play this up and make it a mystifying magic routine.

You don't have to be in the kitchen to perform this. You can be at school, the park, a friend's house, or riding in the car. This is a really fun trick to play anywhere.

A Prediction Trick

THE TRICK

This is a great trick and not that hard. Don't let the fact that you have to add and subtract keep you from learning it! You ask someone to give you three numbers. After some simple math you arrive at the number 9, which matches your **prediction**. Amazing!

HOW DO YOU DO IT?

If you do the math correctly, their answer will always be the number 9.

WHAT YOU NEED

• Pencil
• Scratch paper

PRACTICE TIME

STEP 1

First, let's learn the simple math for this trick. Write down any three numbers. Note: they must be different. No two numbers can be the same.

Let's say you choose 725.

STEP 2

Now reverse the numbers and subtract the smaller number from the larger number. Write your answer down.

725 - 527 = 198

STEP 3

Now add the three numbers in the answer together.

1 + 9 + 8 = 18

STEP 4

Then add the remaining numbers together.

1 + 8 = 9

No matter what numbers you chose at the start, your answer will always be 9.

IT'S SHOWTIME!

Write the number 9 on a piece of paper, fold it up, and put it in your magic box along with the pencil and paper.

Say, "And now it's time for magic with numbers." Bring out the folded prediction (the piece of paper with "9" on it) and ask someone, "Would you please hold on to this?"

Hand your helper a pencil and paper. Say, "I would like you to write down three numbers between one and nine. Each number must be different."

Say, "Now please reverse the numbers, and subtract the smaller number from the larger number." When they have done so, say "Please add each number in the total together until you end up with a single number."

Say, "What is your final number?" They will say, "Nine."

Now ask them to unfold your prediction, and they will be amazed to find that it matches their number.

Say, "Thank you very much. If I was old enough to play the lottery, I could be rich!"

TRY THIS

You can make this trick more
fun by using a balloon, black
marker, and paperclip instead of
pencil and paper.

Before you begin, write the
number 9 on a small piece of paper.
Fold it up small enough to fit inside
the balloon. Grab a permanent black
marker and you are ready to go.

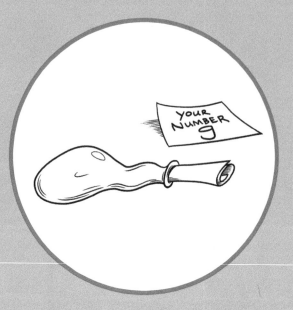

Bring out the balloon and blow it
up. Tie it off. Shake the balloon
and say, "Inside this balloon is
my prediction."

When the audience gives you
numbers, write them on the outside
of the balloon near the top.

Say, "Now we will reverse the numbers and subtract to create a new number."

Now, "I'll add the numbers up to come up with a single number."

Add the numbers up until you get the number nine.

Say, "Your final number is nine."

Now bring out a paperclip, and ask your helper to pop the balloon with the end of the paperclip.

Pick up the paper prediction and show them that your number matches their number

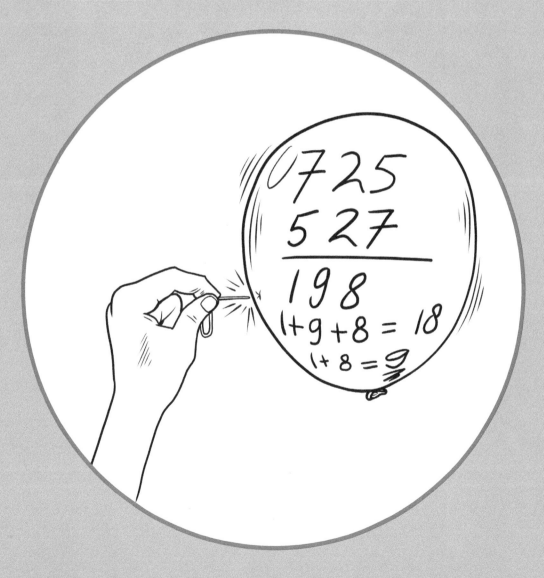

☆ STARGAZING MAGIC ☆

Magic with Numbers

THE TRICK

Ask someone to think of a number on one of four cards. They hand you the cards that have their number and you instantly know what number they are thinking of.

HOW DO YOU DO IT?

Each card has a key number in the center. You add up the center number on the cards and you will instantly know their number.

WHAT YOU NEED

- A sheet of paper or cardboard
- A marker, pen, or pencil
- Scissors

MAKING THE PROPS

Cut out four stars from the paper or cardboard. Now write the numbers just like they are shown here. It's important that the key numbers 1, 2, 4, and 8 are written in the center so you can easily locate them. If you don't want to cut stars, you can cut squares.

PRACTICE TIME

We will first practice this on ourselves and get really good at doing it.

STEP 1

Choose a number from 1 to 16. Let's say our number is 11.

STEP 2

Now, find all the stars that have the number 11 on them and put them in a pile.

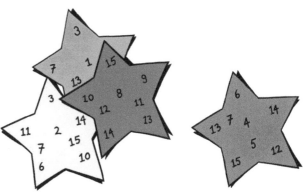

STEP 3

Now add up the numbers in the center on those stars in the pile. You should have stars with center numbers 8, 2, and 1. That will make the total 11. It works every time.

STEP 4

Try it again with the number 6. Then try it with number 15.

Practice this until you can add up the numbers quickly.

IT'S SHOWTIME!

Bring out the four stars from your magic box and say, "The stars tell me that it's time for some magic with numbers."

Ask your helper to think of a number from 1 to 16. Give them a few seconds to think of it. (Let's say they choose 15.)

Say, "Have you got a number?" When they say yes, hand them the stars and tell them to give you back the stars that have their number written on them.

Now, remember what we did in practice time. When they hand you the stars, you add up the center numbers in your head. Before you say their number, tell them *thank you* for helping out. Say, "And now, I will look at the stars and divine the number you are thinking of."

Hold a star up above your head and stare at it. Keep gazing at the star and say, "Aha! It's slowly becoming clear. I see one number, one number that's brighter than all the others. I see the number . . . 15!" This is another trick you can repeat. Maybe ask someone else to think of a number and perform it with them.

TRY THIS

Make these stars using different-colored paper, or use markers to color each one. With practice, you will know which number is in the center by looking at the color of the star. Tell your helper to put the stars facedown on the table, and by looking at the colors, you know what numbers to add up in your head.

If you can't find colored paper, try making them out of different shapes. You can easily identify your number by the shape of each card.

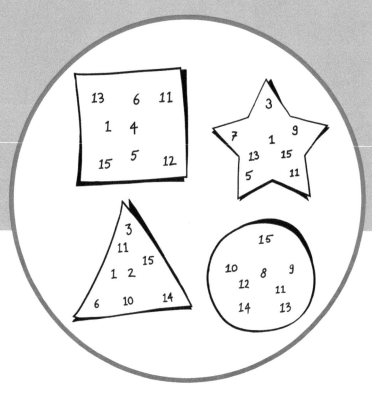

☆ MAGNETIC FINGER ☆

Rising Cards with the Touch of Your Finger

THE TRICK

You rub your finger on your sleeve and then tap the cards, and the chosen card rises up by magic.

HOW DO YOU DO IT?

The secret is your pinkie (baby) finger does the work.

WHAT YOU NEED

• A deck of playing cards. Find a deck that fits your hands comfortably.

PRACTICE TIME
STEP 1

Hold the deck of cards in your hand, wrapping your fingers around in front and thumb in back. Now make a fist with your other hand, and extend your index finger like you are pointing to someone. Hold your hand behind the deck with your finger on top.

STEP 2

Secretly extend your little pinkie finger and press it against the card.

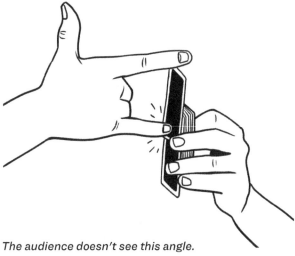

The audience doesn't see this angle.

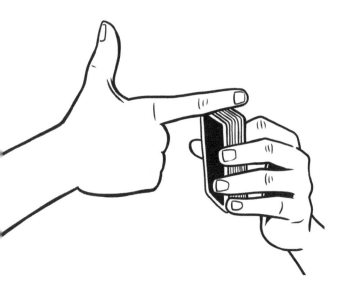

STEP 3

Keep applying pressure with your pinkie finger and raise your hand up. With practice, you can easily cause the card to move straight up. Be sure not to squeeze the deck so hard that the card doesn't slide.

The illusion is that the card is attracted to your finger.

STEP 4

Make the card rise up about half-way, then stop when the card is just a little over halfway up.

Now grab the card with your finger and thumb and remove it.

Be sure to practice this one in front of a mirror so the audience doesn't see your pinkie in back.

This is what the audience sees.

IT'S SHOWTIME!

Bring out the deck of cards, and hold them in your left hand as you did in practice.

Hold up your first finger, look at it for a moment, and blow on it. This will create mystery. Tell your audience, "Watch this."

Now cause the card to rise up about halfway. Then stop when the card is just a little over halfway up. You can make an eerie sound with your voice to create a little mystery. Now grab the card, hand it out, and place it on the table. Blow on your finger again, and repeat one or two more times. Now look at the audience, smile, and say, "Magic finger!"

☆ THE CROSS-CUT FORCE ☆

A Simple Prediction Using a Card Force

THE TRICK

Your helper picks a card, and it matches your **prediction**.

HOW DO YOU DO IT?

You **force** the helper to pick the card in a sneaky way. The Cross-Cut Force is an important skill to learn that you can apply to many card tricks. Let's learn how it's done, and then we'll learn a few card tricks that make use of it.

WHAT YOU NEED

- A deck of cards
- A piece of paper and pen to write your prediction

PRACTICE TIME

STEP 1

Get a sheet of paper and write your prediction:

You will choose the eight of clubs.

Fold the paper in half, and in half again. Draw a "?" on the outside. Place your prediction on the table.

STEP 2

Place the deck on the table and cut off the top half of the cards and place them to the left of the bottom pile. You now have two piles: A and B. Be sure to keep track of which pile has the force card on top (it will be B). When you perform this trick, your helper will be doing the cutting, but for practice you will assume that role.

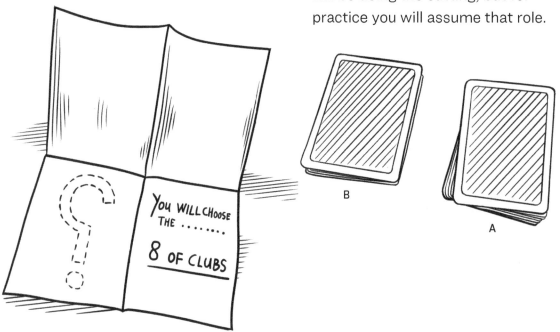

Take the eight of clubs out of the deck and place it on top of the deck. You are going to force the eight of clubs.

STEP 3

Now pick up the bottom half (A) and rotate it a quarter turn, then set it on top of the pile you just cut off (B). The eight of clubs should be on top of pile B.

STEP 4

Pick up your prediction paper and show the "?" on the front. Say, "This is my prediction that I wrote earlier today." Set the prediction back down on the table.

STEP 5

Now pick up pile (A) and point to the top card of pile (B). Here you will ask the spectator to take the top card and turn it over.

(Shh, don't tell them, but your helper will think this is the card they had cut to—when in fact, it's the card you put on top of the deck.)

You have just forced the eight of clubs. And of course, it will match your prediction.

IT'S SHOWTIME!

Say, "Now it's time for a card trick." Bring the cards out and set them on your table.

"Who would like to help me?" When you have chosen a helper, tell them, "Thank you for volunteering.

"Please cut off some cards and set them here on the table." Point to where you want them to place the pile. After they have done that, say, "Thank you."

You now pick up the cards that were on the bottom and turn them a quarter turn and set them on top of the pile that the helper removed.

Call attention to your prediction paper and say, "This is my prediction that I wrote earlier today."

Reach over and pick up the top pile of cards as you did in practice. Point to the card on top of the bottom pile and tell your helper to turn over the card.

They will turn over the card you forced. Say, "You cut to the eight of clubs!"

Now, have the helper pick up your prediction and read it.

When they read your prediction, get ready to take a bow. Thank your helper and tell the audience, "Please give my helper a big round of applause."

TRY THIS

Here are two other ways to reveal the card to your helper.

LOOK UNDER THE MAT Get two eight of clubs cards. Put one under the mat on your table. The other card is on top of the deck. Instead of having a prediction written out, you can proceed with the trick. And when they turn over their card, you say, "Believe it or not, I knew you would choose the eight of clubs." Tell your helper to look under the mat. They will be surprised to find the card matches.

SLEIGHT OF FOOT Hide the second card in your shoe. When they turn over their card, you say, "Believe it or not, I knew you would choose the eight of clubs. I used sleight of foot!" Now reach down, take off your shoe, pull the card out, and show it.

☆ WHISPERING QUEEN ☆

**The Queen
of Hearts Speaks**

THE TRICK

Your helper cuts to a card. You put the queen of hearts up to your ear, and she whispers the name of the card that was cut to.

HOW DO YOU DO IT?

It's all acting on your part. You already know the card because you **forced** it. You pretend the queen is whispering in your ear. This is a great trick to practice your **showmanship**, which is the ability of the magician to capture the audience's attention and to entertain them.

WHAT YOU WILL NEED

• A deck of cards

PRACTICE TIME

This trick requires that you have mastered the Cross-Cut Force from the previous trick. If you have not learned about how to force a card, then read about it on page 89.

Here we will practice some acting skills, pretending the queen is whispering in our ear.

STEP 1

Remove the queen of hearts from the deck, and set it on the table in front of you.

Do the Cross-Cut Force with your helper, forcing the six of clubs. Then ask your helper to pick up the card that you have forced, but tell them not to show it to you. They will think they're picking up the card that they cut to, but you know that it will be the six of clubs.

STEP 2

Hold the queen up to your ear, look up toward the ceiling, and pretend she is telling you the color of the card. Since you know the card is black, say, "She says the card is black. Is that right?" Of course, your helper will say "yes."

STEP 3

Say, "Oh wait a minute, the queen is telling me that your card is a club. Is that right?"

You can compliment the queen for doing a good job.

STEP 4

Look at the queen and say, "What is the value?" Hold it up to your ear, smile, and nod. Now look at your helper and say, "The queen says your card is the six of clubs." Have your helper show you the card to confirm.

IT'S SHOWTIME!

Remove the queen and place it in your magic box.

Put the card you are going to force on top of the deck. Don't forget what the card is! Set the deck on your table. Ask for a helper and tell the audience to give them a round of applause.

Now perform the Cross-Cut Force you learned. Have your helper take the card they cut to (which, of course, is secretly the card you placed on top of the deck), look at it, and place it on the table facedown. Be sure you don't see it.

Say, "I have a friend I want to introduce to you." Bring out the queen of hearts from your magic box. "Please meet my friend, the queen of hearts." Hold the queen to your ear and give them your best acting abilities that you practiced earlier.

TRY THIS

You can add some humor and blindfold the queen or cover her eyes with your hand when the helper is looking at the card they selected. Of course, you should close your eyes so you can't see, either.

Here's another cool idea. Instead of using the queen, why not draw an eye on a small piece of paper and pretend the eye can see all?

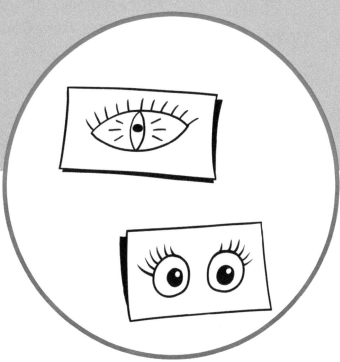

☆ A COMICAL PREDICTION ☆

Your Prediction Unfolds to Reveal Their Card

THE TRICK
Your helper selects a card. You show your prediction, but it's not right. Then you slowly unfold your prediction to reveal you really did predict their card.

HOW DO YOU DO IT?
You have folded your prediction so that it changes each time you open it up.

WHAT YOU NEED
• A deck of cards
• Paper
• A red marker

MAKING THE PROPS
STEP 1

Get a sheet of printer paper and cut it in half so you have two pieces that are 4.25 inches by 11 inches. Fold one piece of paper into four equal pieces. Open it up and draw three diamonds with your red marker at the three folds you made.

STEP 2

Now, fold the right side in and draw the part of the diamond that is not there.

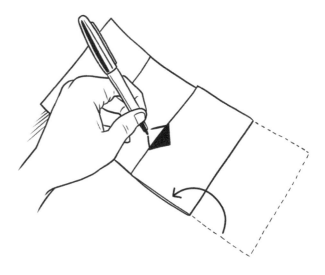

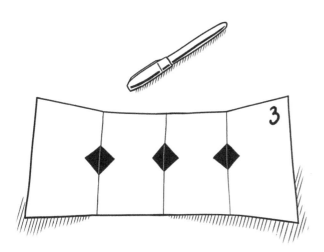

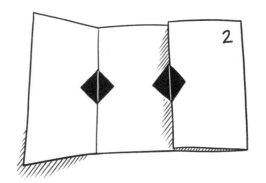

STEP 3

Fold the right side over to the left again and complete the diamond that's missing.

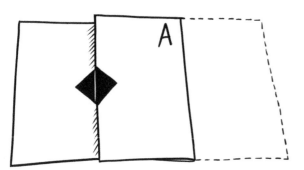

STEP 4

Fold the left side over, covering the diamond, and draw a "?" on it. This is your prediction.

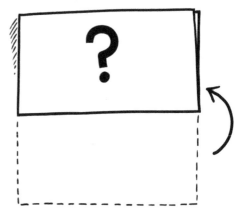

PRACTICE TIME

This trick requires that you have mastered the Cross-Cut Force. If you have not learned about how to force a card, then read the Cross-Cut Force on page 89.

Now look at your prediction paper you made and open it up, one fold at a time, and you can see how it changes from one diamond to two diamonds and finally to three diamonds. Fold it back up and open it again.

IT'S SHOWTIME!

Put the three of diamonds on the top of the deck and you are ready to go.

Force the three of diamonds using the Cross-Cut Force. Tell your helper to look at the card they cut to, but not to show it to you.

Say, "I made a prediction." Show the "?" on your prediction, then open it up to show the one diamond. Say, "Is your card the ace of diamonds?" They will say, "No." Say, "I knew that."

Open up your prediction to show the two of diamonds. Say, "Is your card the two of diamonds?"

They will again say, "No." Say, "I knew that, too." That will get a nice laugh.

Open your prediction again, show the three of diamonds, and say, "Is your card the three of diamonds?" They will say, "Yes." Say, "I knew that!"

☆ I ♥ U ☆

**A Card Trick
Your Parents Will Love**

WHAT IT LOOKS LIKE

You show three cards. Together they spell MOM. (This trick can also be easily changed so that the cards spell DAD, SIS, BRO, or even YOU—whatever name you choose.) You then set the cards down on the table. Have your helper turn over the middle card and to their surprise, it has a special message written just for them.

HOW IT WORKS

One card is **gimmicked** and is hiding your special message.

WHAT YOU NEED

• Four index cards, measuring 3 inches by 5 inches
• Scissors
• Clear tape
• Some crayons or colored markers

MAKING THE PROPS
STEP 1

Take three cards and draw on them with a black marker as shown here. Make two cards with the letter *M* and one card with the letter *O* (again, you can use any three-letter word or name you want, but for these instructions, we'll just assume you're using "MOM").

STEP 2

Cut the *O* card along the dotted line as shown. You will only use the left half of this card. Recycle the right half. Now get a piece of clear tape about 3″ long, and tape the long edge of the *O* card to one of the *M* cards so that about a third of the card on the left is exposed. You have now created your **gimmicked** card.

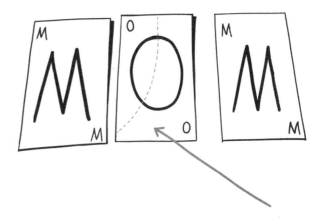

Throw this half (on the right) away.

STEP 4

Now turn over the card that you just drew a heart on and write a message. Here the message says, "Happy Birthday Mom." Be creative and come up with your own message.

STEP 3

Now turn over *M* card that has the flap you just taped and draw the letter *U*. On the other side of the remaining *M* card, draw the letter *I*. On the fourth and remaining card, draw a heart.

PRACTICE TIME
STEP 1
Now let's set the cards up in the right order. Take the card you just wrote "Happy Birthday Mom" on, and slide it under the *O* flap in the gimmicked card you just made.

STEP 2
Place the other *M* card on top of the message card and make sure the edge of the flap is covered. You now have a fan of three cards, with the secret message card hidden under the *O* flap and second *M*. If you're holding the cards correctly, no one will know that the O card isn't a full card.

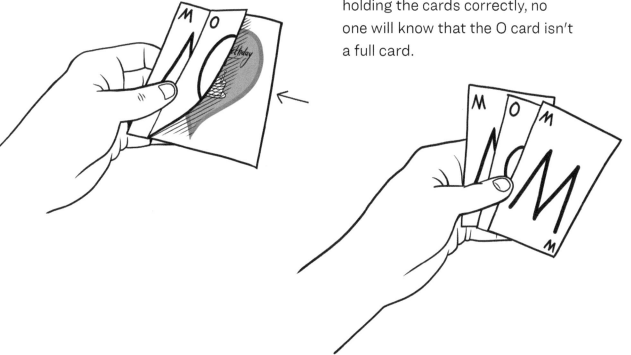

STEP 3

Display the cards, holding them in your left hand with your thumb on top and the fingers behind. With your right hand, grasp the top card (the letter *M*) and place it on the table, turning it over.

STEP 4

Place the next card (the secret message card, which your helper will think is the *O*) down on the table to the left of the first card you put down. Finally, place the last card down (the last *M* with the *O* flap taped to it) to the left of the previous card. You will now see *I* ♥ *U*.

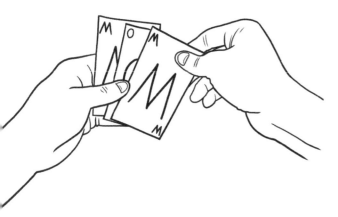

STEP 5

Slowly turn over the middle card to show your message has magically appeared.

IT'S SHOWTIME!

Tell your mom that you have a wonderful surprise for her. Bring out the cards from your magic box, holding them in your left hand.

Say, "Mom, this card trick is special, just like you are. I am holding three cards, spelling the word 'MOM.' I'll put them on the table, and you can see that they now say, 'I love you.'"

Deal the cards down on the table as you did in practice.

Say, "Mom, I have a message from my heart to your heart." Now wave your hands over the cards on the table and say, "I love you!"

Ask your mom to turn over the heart card. Your mom will probably give you a big hug and kiss!

☆ THE MAGIC CYLINDER ☆

Make Objects Appear Out of Thin Air

THE TRICK

After showing the audience an empty paper tube, you **produce** objects out of thin air.

HOW DO YOU DO IT?

The tube has a cleverly disguised empty space where items are secretly hidden.

WHAT YOU NEED

- Two sheets of poster size paper—about 12 inches by 18 inches. The paper should be poster board stiff and the same color.
- Clear tape
- Scissors
- Construction paper or decorations of your choice
- Glue
- Some small objects to produce: colorful scarves, wrapped candy, the rope you used in Knots Impossible, string, and maybe some playing cards

MAKING THE PROPS
STEP 1
Take one sheet of poster board, roll it into a tube, and secure it with clear tape.

STEP 2
Cut the second sheet about 2 inches shorter in length and roll it into a cone shape so one end is the same size as the tube you just made. One end of the cone should be a few inches smaller than its other end.

STEP 3
Insert the tapered cone inside the large cylinder, and tape the wide ends together. Then, tape one side of the narrow end to the outer tube. Trim off the end of the smaller tube if it is too long.

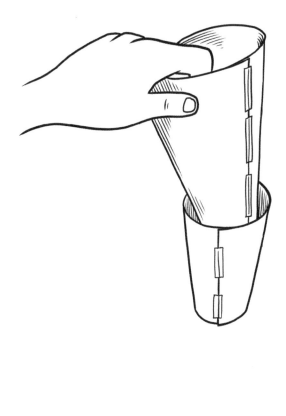

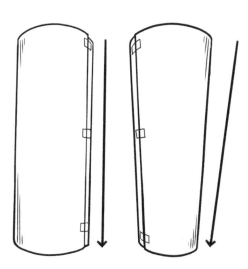

STEP 4

For fun, cut out some stars, moons, and other interesting shapes and glue them to the outside of the cylinder, or draw some fancy designs on the tube. Now let's get practicing.

PRACTICE TIME
STEP 1

Look at the end that has space between the two tubes. This is the magician's secret space where you hide your **production** items, such as rope, string, scarves, and maybe a few playing cards. Carefully stuff them inside below the edge so no one sees them.

STEP 2

Hold up the tube vertically and look through it. Move the tube over to your left side and then over to your right side so everyone is able to see through it. Practice in the mirror so you can see what the audience sees.

STEP 3

Now, place the tube down on your table with the secret space up. Wave your wand over the tube and say the magic word, "Alakazam."

STEP 4

Reach in and slowly produce the items one at a time, holding them up high so everyone can see. Set them on the table around the tube. Congratulations! You've just made your first magical production.

IT'S SHOWTIME!

This illusion is a good one to end your show with. It's flashy and eye-catching. Make sure that no one is behind you when you perform this.

Say, "I've enjoyed performing for you today, and I want to end with something big. It's time for the grand finale." Now hold up the tube so everyone can see through it. Say, "As you can see, this tube is empty. Nothing here at all."

Place the tube on your table. Say, "Everyone please hold up your hands, wiggle your fingers, and say, *something from nothing*."

Now produce the colorful scarves you stored inside and set them down on your table. Wait for the audience to go *ooh* and *ah*. Finally, dump out the wrapped candy and pass it out to everyone.

Take a bow and say, "That's the show, thank you!"

TRY THIS

You can also begin the magic show by producing your magic props from the tube. Say, "It's showtime! But, first I need my props." Then bring out the tube, say the magic word "Alakazam!" and produce the props from inside.

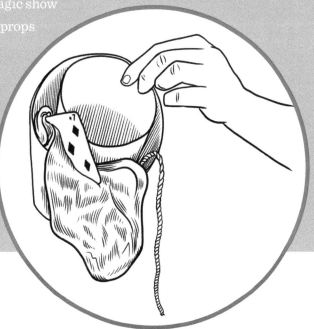

QUICK TRICKS AND PRACTICAL JOKES

MAGIC MARKER

This is a fun joke that always gets a laugh. It can be presented in the middle of your show.

Take a black marker out of your magic box, and hold it up so everyone can see it. Tell the audience that this marker can write in any color. Now, ask your helper to name a color. Let's says they name blue. Put a mysterious look on your face and wave your hand over the marker.

Say the magic word, "Abracadabra." Now hold up the marker and say, "This marker now writes blue." Your audience will be puzzled. Now, pick up a piece of paper and write the word "BLUE." Smile and take a bow.

JUST SAY NO

Here's another one. Tell your helper you have written a prediction on a slip of paper. Show the back of the paper, but make sure no one can see through it. Now ask, "Do you know what is written on this paper?" When they say no, turn the paper around and say, "You are correct!"

What you have done is write the word "NO" on the card ahead of time. You'll hear lots of laughter and maybe a few groans.

BET-CHA CAN'T DO IT

Hand someone a piece of paper and say, "I bet you can't tear this into four pieces. If you can, I'll give you a quarter." Your helper will know they are easily up for the task and will tear the paper into four pieces. Act surprised and say, "Oh wow, you did it." Now, hand them one of the four pieces and say, "Here's your quarter!" Get it? Your helper thought you were going to give them a quarter, 25 cents.

TWO COIN PUZZLE

Hold a penny and a quarter in your hand. Shake them and say, "I have two coins in my hand. The total is 26 cents. Both are American coins, but one is not a penny. What are the two coins?"

After your audience gives up, open your hand and show the quarter and the penny. Hold up the quarter and say, "This one is not a penny." Most people assumed you were saying that neither one is a penny.

PRONOUNCE IT

This gets them every time. Ask someone to pronounce T-O-P. Then ask them to pronounce H-O-T. Now ask them to pronounce P-O-T. Now ask them, "What do you do when you come to a green light?" And it's a sure thing they will say, "STOP." Tell them, "No you don't—you go!"

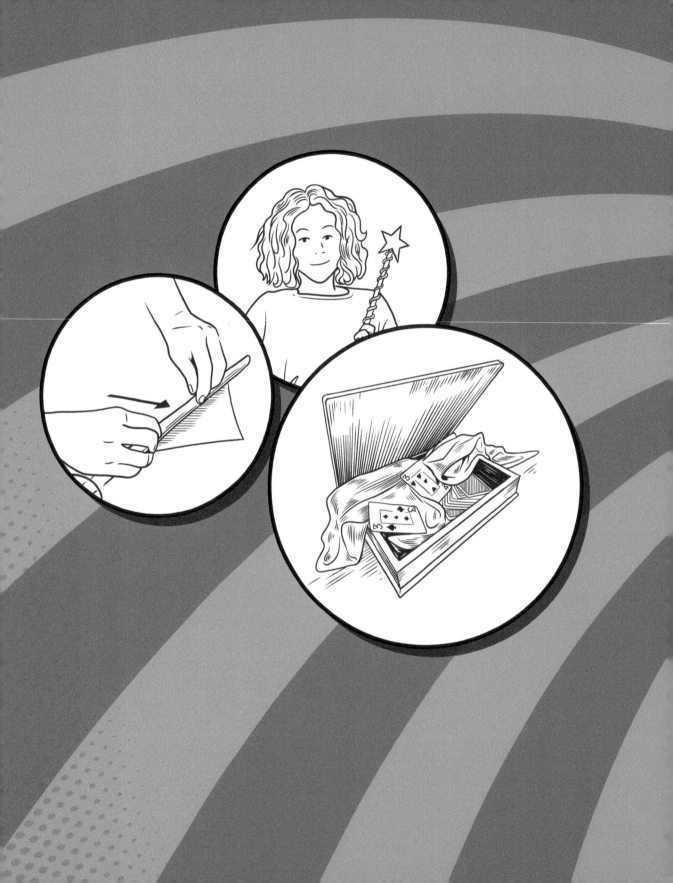

MAGICAL CRAFTS

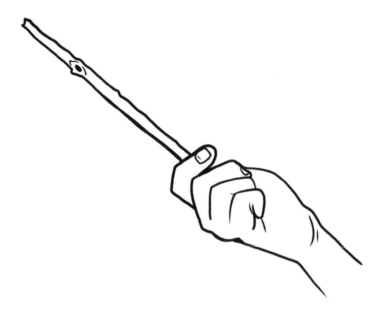

MAGIC WAND

The magic wand can be used to help make the magic happen. Waving the wand creates excitement and suspense for the audience. Wands also help serve as **misdirection** tools, causing the audience to look where the magician wants them to look.

The black magic wand with a white tip was made popular by French magician Jean Robert-Houdin. The wand he used measured about 13 to 14 inches in length and was made from expensive wood called ebony with rounded ends made from ivory. Other wands were carved from special wood and had expensive jewels attached to them.

But magic wands don't have to be this fancy. Anything can become a magic wand. You can use a small tree branch or a long round piece of wood. It can be colorful or plain.

FIND SMALL OBJECTS AROUND THE HOUSE

Make your wand with objects found around the home or outside. Your wand could be a pencil, ruler, tree branch, chopstick, or even a wooden spoon.

A magic wand made from a chopstick , tape, and construction paper.

How to make a paper wand

Take a piece of construction paper and roll it from one end to the other. Secure the loose end with some tape. Then take some chenille stems (pipe cleaners) and wrap them around the tightly rolled paper. Be creative and design a magic wand that suits you.

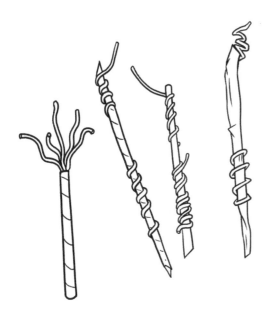

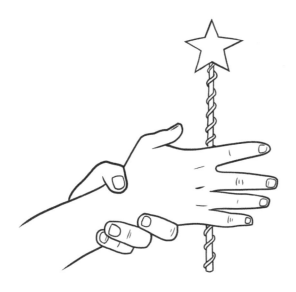

IDEAS FOR USING YOUR MAGIC WAND

- Use it to make the straw roll across the table in Straw Sorcery.
- Use your magic wand for the Magnetic Hand trick.
- Put your wand inside the Magic Cylinder to show it is empty.

MAGIC BOX

Keep all your magic **props** in one place so you can find them when you need them. Ask your parents if they have a box with a lid large enough to store all the magic that you make and gather. A shoebox or a gift box will do just fine. You can also go to a craft or hobby shop to buy a wooden box. Ask your family to help you paint it. If the box is plain, then you can be creative and decorate it. Cover it with colorful paper or draw on it with markers or crayons. Cut out shapes, such as stars, and glue them to your box.

MAGIC TABLE

A magic table can help you put on a fantastic magic show. It's where you can store your props (maybe in your magic box!), and provides a good surface for you to perform tricks on. Here's a simple table you can make with just a couple of cardboard boxes and a sheet or blanket. Ask your parents for a couple of empty moving boxes or file boxes. Stack one box on the other, then cover them with the blanket.

Put a mat on top. You can use a table placemat or dish towel. Draw your name on a sheet of paper and tape it or use safety pins to attach it to the blanket in front of your new table. You're now ready to put on a show!

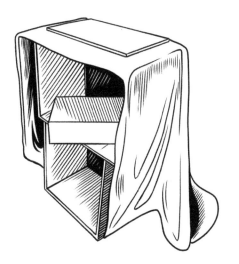

BECOMING A GREAT MAGICIAN

Now that you've been practicing your magic, here are a few tips that will help you become a truly great magician.

PRACTICE

It bears repeating: Never stop practicing. Set time aside every day to practice your new skills and know your **patter** by heart. Practice in front of a mirror to make sure the audience doesn't see the objects hidden in your hands. Stand up straight, smile, and relax. As you continue to practice over time, you will become more comfortable and you will gain confidence. A great magician is confident with their magic and is comfortable performing in front of their audience. They spend hours and hours polishing their craft to delight their audiences. And you can, too.

FIND YOUR STYLE

As you continue practicing, you will develop your own personal style— the thing that makes you YOU. For some of these tricks, it might be fun to make your voice sound mysterious. Raise one eyebrow and make a funny face. Create some drama and excitement with how you move, how you talk, or how you react to the magic. Wear a cool hat that fits your style. The audience will enjoy seeing you do this and will enjoy your magic more.

PUT ON A SHOW

You may want to consider putting on a magic show. Set up a spot in the room with plenty of space for you to stand. This is your stage. Set up the **magic table** from page 125 or ask your parents if you can borrow a small folding table. Arrange chairs for the audience to sit and watch. You may want to play some music in the background as they come in to sit down. Have your magic props set up and ready to go in your **magic box**.

CREATE A ROUTINE

A professional magician creates routines, stringing together two or more tricks in a row, one following the other. This is easy to do. First, find the tricks that you are really good at and put them together in a "playlist" of tricks, so one trick easily flows into the next. Be sure to practice your routine—doing one trick after the other from start to finish.

Here are some tricks you can do for a fun-filled show. Create your own routines with the tricks that you have mastered.

Playlist for Beginner Magicians
Meet Mr. Zippy
Straw Sorcery
Magnetic Hand
Caught Red-Handed
Jack the Jolly Jumping Rubber Band
Linking Paper Clips

Playlist for Intermediate Magicians
Multiplying Money II
Don't Cry, George!
Coin in Elbow
Color Vision
Levitating Latte

Playlist for Advanced Magicians

The Magic Cylinder—produce the items for the next tricks in your show

Knots Impossible

Amazing String Trick

Stargazing Magic

I ♥ U

WHEN SOMETHING GOES WRONG

Every magician will have a trick go wrong in their show. It happens to all of us. What do you do when a trick goes wrong? Sometimes there is no way to recover—it's just best to put the trick away and move on to the next trick. When you have put together a playlist, it will give you a better chance of recovering when a trick fails. You can just look up at your audience, smile, and say, "Let's move on to the next trick in the show." For example, if you drop the coin on the floor, just pick it up and keep going. If you force the wrong card, don't worry, just put the cards away and show them something else more amazing.

Here are a few other lines you can memorize and say when a trick fails. Smile and say:

"You all look lovely tonight."

"I bet you want to see my next trick. Yeah, me too!"

"Well, that trick didn't go as planned, but hey, I finished my homework!"

"Hey, I don't want you to get your expectations up too high!"

"Gee whiz, that's the first time that's happened . . . AGAIN!"

FINALLY

Congratulations on your new skill. Using magic to make people laugh and smile is a wonderful thing. Have fun along the way and your audiences will have fun, too. Learning to do magic is an incredible journey that I have been on my whole life. I know you will experience great success, too. You can learn more about magic at the following places:

Your local library: Visit your library and head on over to section 793.8. That's where you will find books on magic tricks and illusions. There is a wealth of information waiting for you there.

Society of Young Magicians: This organization is part of the Society of American Magicians and is devoted to helping magicians ages 7 to 17 in the art of magic. More information is available at MagicSam.com/page/SYMYouthProgram.

GLOSSARY

animation: This is when the magician is able to make objects move by themselves, such as making a handkerchief dance inside a bottle or making Mr. Zippy come to life.

close-up: This is magic that is done up close for a small group of people. The magician usually works at a table or can stroll around the room carrying the magic tricks in their pockets. Multiplying Money I and II are good examples of close-up magic.

force: In card magic, the magician asks the helper to pick a card. The helper thinks they have a free choice, but the magician is forcing them to take the card the magician wants them to take.

gimmicked: A gimmicked card is one that has been changed in some way to help a magician perform a trick. It looks like a normal card, but it often has a secret or "gimmick."

illusion: This is when something looks real but is not. The word "illusion" sometimes refers to large-scale magic done onstage. The famous magician David Copperfield performs illusions onstage in his Las Vegas show.

impromptu: This is when the magician is able to perform magic with little or no time to prepare. If you ask a magician to do a trick, and they pull a coin out of their pocket and make it disappear, then they are doing impromptu magic.

levitate: The ability to make an object or person rise up or float in midair, defying the laws of gravity.

mentalist: When a magician says that they have the power to read minds, they are sometimes referred to as a mentalist. They are sometimes called a "mind reader."

misdirection: This is what the magician says or does that will direct the audience's attention to where the magician wants them to look.

patter: The words that magicians say when they are performing. Sometimes this is called a "script." It can be a story, instructions, or questions the magician will ask.

penetration: This is when a magician makes one solid object pass through another solid object. This is what we learn when we make the metal paper clips seemingly link together.

prediction: This is the magician's ability to know in advance what someone is thinking or that something is about to occur, such as what card will be selected or what number someone is thinking of.

production: A production is the effect when a magician makes something appear, for example, producing handkerchiefs out of an empty box.

props: The equipment the magician needs to perform their magic. These can be playing cards, coins, and also a table or boxes needed in their act.

showmanship: This is the ability of the magician to capture the audience's attention and to entertain them.

sleight of hand: The secret skills the magician uses to make the magic happen. The sleight of hand is not seen by the audience. A magician that is skillful in sleight of hand can make objects appear, disappear, and change places with just their bare hands.

suspension: This is when the magician is able to make something stay in the air and not fall. This is similar to levitation, where objects defy gravity, but here the object is suspended and it doesn't float up or away from the magician.

switch: When magicians want to secretly exchange one item for another, such as a coin or card or even a person hiding in a box, they call that a switch. This can be similar to a transformation or transposition.

transposition: This is when a magician makes one or more objects move from one place to another. In the Jack the Jolly Jumping Rubber Band trick, the magician makes the rubber band move from one finger to a different finger.

vanish: When a magician makes objects disappear, it's called a vanish.

voila!: This is a French word often said at the end of tricks that means, "Here it is!"

ACKNOWLEDGMENTS

I must acknowledge the thousands of kids who have taken my magic classes at schools, libraries, camps, and private parties. I thank Joseph Bradley and James Tedrow, who have assisted me at the many workshops I have put on.

Thanks to aspiring magicians, eight-year-old Gunnar and my seven-year-old nephew, Bennett, for practicing the tricks and providing valuable feedback on some of the new material.

My friend and fellow magician Ormond McGill, who was the first author of magic books I met.

To my Aunt Louise, a Palo Alto librarian, whose love of books instilled in me the excitement and desire to explore the secrets found between their covers. Little did I know way back in the 1960s that I would turn my avocation into a vocation and perform at libraries, sharing both my excitement about reading and my love of magic with today's youth.

And to all the magicians who came before me whose teachings inspired my thinking and gave me the desire to become a successful magician.

And finally, my family. My dad, who bought me my first books on magic and drove me to the House of Magic in San Francisco. My mom, who sewed costumes and table covers and was always telling me to stand up straight when performing. And my sister, having to put up with the excitement of her brother demanding, "Hey, Julie, come watch this!"

ABOUT THE AUTHOR

Phil Ackerly (MakePhilAppear.com) is a magician, speaker, and storyteller who has performed over 10,000 shows in his 40-year career. He graduated with a degree in electronics and worked for 15 years in the high-tech industry in Silicon Valley. In 1992, he decided to pursue a full-time career in magic.

Phil has won multiple awards in close-up, parlor, and stage magic, and has performed all over the country, including at the Magic Castle in Hollywood, California, and off-Broadway in New York City at Monday Night Magic.

Phil is a member of the Society of American Magicians, the International Brotherhood of Magicians (IBM), and The Oakland Magic Circle. He is an active member of the Society of American Magicians, Silicon Valley Assembly #94, serving as its president.

Phil conducts workshops for schools, libraries, summer camps, and private parties, giving him the wealth of information that makes up this, his first published book on magic.

Phil lives in Santa Clara, California.

CPSIA information can be obtained
at www.ICGtesting.com
Printed in the USA
JSHW022114281121
20791JS00002B/3